Critical Theory

Critical Theory

Matthew Manus

iUniverse, Inc.

New York Lincoln Shanghai

Critical Theory

iUniverse, Inc.

For information address:
iUniverse, Inc.
2021 Pine Lake Road, Suite 100
Lincoln, NE 68512
www.iuniverse.com

ISBN: 0-595-32890-3

Printed in the United States of America

Contents

Introduction

This critical theory is my contribution to the critique of capitalism and the effects of capitalism upon the human individual and society.

Matthew Manus
August 2004
Saint Louis, MO USA

Adceleration

Adceleration describes the process by which the media speeds up time in the mind of the human individual. For example, television shows often compress years into an hour or less. This creates in the mind of the human individual an adcelerated perception of time.

Adeptition

Adeptition describes the idea that capitalism creates consumers of goods and that capitalistic forces engineer the desires for those goods.

Aestheticfaction

Aestheticfaction describes the media's manufacturing of aesthetics to which all humans are expected to adhere. This exploitation of aesthetics is inherently destructive and leads to the manufacturing of unnatural desires.

Aesthetic Transformatorics

Aesthetic transformatorics describes the process whereby contexts are permuted throughout various aesthetics. This process is a fundamental property of the human mind. Capitalism engineers aesthetics and contexts and it can be said that capitalism is in control of contemporary aesthetic transformatorics.

Anthropusation

Anthropusation is the idea that humans elevate themselves above all things in order to gain control of their psychological and ecological environments.

Capitalectics

Capitalectics describes the idea that capitalist forces have inherent contradictions that ultimately contribute to the destruction of the human individual's natural instincts, replacing it with unnatural instincts that leads to unnatural desires.

Contextorics

Contextorics describes the process by which capitalist forces create and permute new contexts for the human individual to exist in, both psychologically and ecologically.

D-Theory

D-Theory is the idea that the human instinct is ultimately what governs human desire. Capitalistic forces are dangerous because they transform humans' instincts, leading to the manufacturing of unnatural desires.

Derelinquation

Derelinquation describes the idea that capitalism causes humans to abandon their moralities in order to justify satisfaction of their desires, some of which are manufactured by capitalistic forces.

Fastigition

Fastigition describes the idea that capitalism promotes itself as the epitome of economic fairness for the human individual.

Fidation

Fidation is the idea that capitalism generates new systems of beliefs in order to derive profit from the human individuals that adhere to them.

G-engineering

G-engineering is the process by which capitalistic forces engineer the behavior of humans around the world.

G-leptics

G-leptics describes the idea that capitalism manufactures the desire within the human individual's mind to integrate with a global aesthetic, constantly in evolution, that leads to greater control of the global media over the human individual's personal aesthetic.

Geoamation

Geoamation is the love of living in the world that capitalism induces by enticing the human subject to believe that life can be improved via the fulfillment of natural (and manufactured) desires.

Hypergerity

Hypergerity describes the process by which the human individual finds the correct intellectual contexts to justify their instinctual drives. Capitalism has increased hypergerity by creating many new intellectual contexts and by manufacturing unnatural instinctual urges. The increase of hypergerity has led to the disintegration of morality in all the geoid's cultures.

Immodication

Immodication is the idea that capitalism treats as abnormal certain humans that do not have a place in the capitalist infrastructure in order to profit off of them.

Law of Appropriation

The law of appropriation states that capitalism appropriates whatever justifies its inherent need to transform human individuals into consumers.

Law of Human Nature

The law of human nature states that all humans want to create optimal circumstances to sustain their intended existence. Capitalism is aware of this law and utilizes its knowledge of it to derive profit from human individuals.

Legacyfaction

Legacyfaction is the idea that capitalistic forces compel people to leave legacies that effect other people. These legacies stem from the innate human desire to remain immortal. It is capitalism that packages these legacies as products and turns legacyfaction into variegated industries. Legacies are both created and consumed.

Legacypositioning

Legacypositioning is the process by which a human individual engineers his/her legacy by utilizing capitalist forces to his/her advantage. A good example of this is the rise to power of a politician. The politician utilizes the media and capital in order to engineer his/her legacy.

Lexicality

Lexicality describes the process by which human nature is conformed to externally imposed laws. Capitalism creates new laws so that it can control the human individual to a greater extent.

Moration

Moration describes the idea that capitalist forces ultimately disintegrate the human individual's innate morality over time and replace it with the capitalist morality. The capitalist morality is in constant flux in regards to changing sets of circumstances, but one thing is constant—the human individual must be a consumer of goods and ideologies.

Mythfaction

Mythfaction describes the process by which mythologies are engineered and utilized by the media in order to control the instinctual drives of the human individual.

Perfiction

Perfiction describes the process by which capitalism tends to define the success of the human individual by their accomplishments rather than their character and morality.

Permutationalistics

Permutationalistics describes the process by which information is permuted throughout various contexts by the human mind as the human mind settles upon the permutation of information that justifies their desires and actions.

Quantumagraphy

Quantumagraphy describes the assignation of names to various 'particles', all of which have mass. Particles without mass are simply constructs that cannot be measured by contemporary technologies and conveniently allow for the solvability of physical equations as well as for the construction of physical theories that require particles without mass in order to be regarded as plausible.

Reconstruction of Everyday Life

The reconstruction of everyday life is the process that all humans go through on a daily basis when they recontextualize the past in order to understand the present and predict the future. The reconstruction of everyday life today is largely engineered by the forces of capitalism.

Scholation

Scholation is the process by which capitalism manufactures new disciplines in the academy in order to exercise greater control over the innate talents of human individuals.

Subition

Subition describes the abrupt paradigm shifts that occur in the academy and the marketplace due to the forces of capitalism needing new ideas and technologies to continue to create profit from humans.

Surfaction

Surfaction describes the idea that capitalist forces engineer the imagination of the human individual by permuting it in unnatural combinations, combinations that ultimately lead people to act and think unnaturally.

Symboleptics

Symboleptics describes the process by which information (imagery, words, etc.) becomes symbolic to a human at a deep psychological level. Symboleptics is used by the media and other capitalistic forces in order to gain control over the human individual's emotions and desires.

0-595-32890-3

www.ingramcontent.com/pod-product-compliance
Lightning Source LLC
Chambersburg PA
CBHW021247280526
45784CB00005B/2273